# BREAKING THE MOLD

*Why Waste Talent?*

*Make a Difference and Prove It Can Be Done by
Your Decisions, Dedication & Determination*

## WILLIAM E. LEE JR.

Copyright © 2013 by William E. Lee Jr.

www.WilliamLeeOnline.com

All rights reserved, including the right to reproduce this book or portion thereof in any form whatsoever.

This document is published by WilliamLeeOnline.com. located in the United States of America. It is protected by the United States Copyright Act, all applicable state laws and international copyright laws. The information in this document is accurate to the best of the ability of the author at the time of writing. The content of this document is subject to change without notice.

For more information regarding special discounts for bulk purchases, please contact Nikkia at: booking@williamleeonline.com

# DEDICATION

First and foremost, I would like to give honor to God for all he has done for me, allowing me to stay on this earth and continuing to make a difference.

My mother, Donna Keesee, for bringing me into this world and molding me into the person I am today, by strictly raising me the right way.

My father, William E. Lee Sr., Thank you for giving me wisdom and insight about life and how to walk and talk like a man.

My loving sister, Kiana Keesee (Your brother loves you).

My grandmothers Ruby Lambert, Marie Lee, & grandfathers Spencer Keesee, and James Lee. Thank you for being such inspiration and making sure I stay focused.

Godmothers, Barbara Jean Hooper and Lutrellia McAllister, I love for you being wonderful Godmothers.

One of the best lifetime friends a man could ever have, Alfred Wooten

Thanks for being great business mentors and associates, Vincent K. Harris, Juan Langford and Robert Allen

# ACKNOWLEDGMENTS

To my heavenly Father who has made this book possible, I give Him all the glory. I'm certainly grateful that I'm not who I used to be, and I can't thank Him enough for giving me a good family as well as supportive mentors. They all want to see me do great things and live a life of value, He made that possible.

To my Mother, thank you for raising me to be the man that I am today. You brought me up as a single mother, and I want to bless you with everything your heart desires. I'm striving to see you happier and enjoying the good life without having to struggle. You've been the best mom and I love you for that.

My grandmother Ruby Reynolds, I remember spending enjoyable nights at your house as a child. You helped raise your grandchildren in a way that was righteous, and provided for our every need. You fed us not only good table food, but good food for thought. Thank you for being a wonderful grandmother.

My grandmother Marie Lee, I love you for always allowing me to be myself. Thank you for your ongoing support and being there when I needed someone to talk to about life. You always made me laugh with your funny jokes. I love you for that!

My father, I became an artist just by watching you as a child. Now, I am applying the knowledge I learned. I appreciate you for encouraging me to pursue my dreams.

My sister Kiana, I love you and I want you to become a great Woman of God that stands on God's word. I will always be your big brother and help you create your legacy.

I would like to thank my church family for always being supportive in my life, and just for being great people.

I would like to thank my editor, Javona Smith, for making my thoughts pleasurable and insightful to read.

Finally, to anyone else whose name I neglected to mention, thank you for everything and let's break the mold together. "Legacy"

# CONTENTS

Introduction.................................................................7

**Chapter One:** Sharing My Message: The Unbelievable Journey................................................................ 10

**Chapter Two**: The Crash......................................... 17

**Chapter Three:** The Entrepreneurial Turnaround........... 21

**Chapter Four:** Get Your Dream Back....................... 28

**Chapter Five:** Ideas Need Leaders............................ 35

**Chapter Six:** The Danger of Giving Up Too Soon.......... 44

**Chapter Seven:** Execution is an Art............................51

**Chapter Eight:** Unlock Your Potential....................... 64

**Chapter Nine:** Breaking the Curse............................ 68

**Chapter Ten:** Why Waste Talent...............................71

**Chapter Eleven:** Mental Success Strategies................... 75

**Chapter Twelve:** Daily Affirmations......................... 78

**About the Author**.................................................81

# INTRODUCTION

This book builds upon several life components:

- ✓ Overcoming adversity by leveraging your gifts and talents, knowledge, sharing wisdom, and learning from your mistakes in life to help increase the quality of someone else's life.

- ✓ Realizing that most things happen because of the poor choices we make. You are on this earth to make a difference, and the only way to make a difference is with your decisions, dedication, and determination.

- ✓ Discovering and understanding your gift to the world, *"Why Waste Talent?"* Your message, gifts and talents can open doors that will sow into your life what you reap. You can break the mold by doing things differently, destroy generational curses, and embracing your uniqueness by completing tasks in such a way that others may not.

There will be times when you must put your blood, sweat and tears into what you believe in. Times you will go through trial and error and even times when you will feel like giving up, but when you finally discover your purpose, it is a life-changing advent. Realize that giving up would be a selfish act and is not an option; you were created to make a difference or, *"Break the Mold"* for the sake of your legacy. Every person on this earth is distinctively different and created with a God-given talent or gift. We all possess the ability to create our own destiny utilizing our respective strengths and weaknesses as well as unique traits and characteristics.

God plants invisible seeds in all of us; these seeds are called dreams. With the faith of a mustard seed, these dreams will flourish and manifest themselves into the physical realm. Aspirations and ambitions are placed on our hearts so that we will strive for the things we want to have, do, and become in our lifetimes. You will be able to help your loved ones and others if you have passion, the will to give your all, good intentions, and consistency. When you possess all of the above, the dreams that are patiently awaiting your arrival will be brought into fruition.

Have you ever had someone try to mold you into something they wanted you to be? There comes a point in your life when you have to find the fit that is right for you. Doing this starts with being yourself, not trying to be anyone else. Follow your dreams and listen to the inner voice that tells says you can do it, and align your thoughts with your gifts and talents. You will then be in the direct position to excel in business while staying true to yourself as well as your dreams.

As an entrepreneur there are many things we want to accomplish at the same time. However, that is a surefire way for an entrepreneur to fail. You have to stay focused on what you want to become successful in before taking on any new projects. Write down what you want to do, write the steps to achieve those goals, and then take action. Success in business requires a well thought-out plan that is written clearly and able to be strategically followed through on.

*Chapter 1*

# SHARING MY MESSAGE: THE UNBELIEVABLE JOURNEY

*The journey of a thousand miles begins with one step.*

– Lao Tzu

Have you ever felt so passionate about something or someone that the situation or that person stayed on your mind constantly? The saying goes, "Never give up on something you can't go a day thinking about." If you stay focused on taking the steps needed to achieve the goals you are passionate about, things will begin to manifest. The reason this happens is because all of your positive energy is pouring into that particular thought. I always knew there was something inside of me that would focus on creating paths and leading others to their God-given purpose – I just did not always know how that would come to be.

I knew the source of my talents; I also knew I have always possessed a leadership mindset. However, I was not always sure how to develop my gifts. Developing your natural gifts and talents comes from the desire to do what you love to do and would do for free; the key is to find a way to help others with your gifts and to capitalize on it. Great leaders today are using their same passion to with new desires, and transforming them into profitable businesses. Many of these leaders started out by working somewhere for free, but in the process they learned a skill and eventually earned a name for themselves.

After gaining a clientele, or after consistently handling business transactions, surely these leaders developed a written plan and ran full speed ahead with their vision. If you must work for someone, do so only to learn something more, to become something better - then work for yourself. Once you get a taste of entrepreneurship, you may never want to quit. In the entrepreneurial world, quitting should never be an option anyway. We will make mistakes, however we must learn from our mistakes and never make the same mistake twice.

As a child, I remember the first time I saw my father drawing; I wanted to know how to draw pictures just like him. I started drawing consistently and I loved it, I was very passionate about it. One day while I was sitting at my grandmother's kitchen table drawing a sailboat in a sea, my mother came out the back room to see what I was doing. She already knew I was artistic, but it wasn't until that moment that she realized how passionate and dedicated I was. Seeing I had potential and could utilize my talents, she said, *"I need to put you in an art class."* Soon after that interaction, I started my first day of class with other artists.

I fell in love with that class instantly; I cannot even explain to you how much I thoroughly enjoyed it. As time went by, I met other artists who were also very passionate about art and good at what they did. I remember meeting my art teacher for the first time and building a strong rapport with her. She was kind, generous, and the coolest person you could ever meet. It felt great to be in such a welcoming, talented, and creative atmosphere with other like-minded artists.

My first art piece was a masterpiece painting of another sailboat in the ocean. At the time, I thought it didn't have any meaning. Now I realize it may have been my vision of easy access to an abundance of joy, immunity from poverty and a sign that I was embarking on a spiritual journey. My family was very proud of me and supportive of my passion, and when I expressed that I needed a nice frame to display my painting, a relative offered to invest in a frame for my painting. I will never forget that kind gesture. It was a bit shocking to me, and it showed me how much my relative saw the value in my work.

After being in class for a few more months, I created more pieces and framed them. But I started to think about how I can capitalize on my drawings and paintings – I came up blank. The interest I once had for drawing and painting, suddenly disappeared. I then decided to tell my mother I no longer wanted to pursue that in which she had already invested so much into for my future. She was disappointed, but supported my decision.

Years later, I dreamed about being an architect, picturing myself the owner of a company with many employees. I quickly dismissed that dream as I knew it would take quite a few years of school to make it a reality. I had an epiphany, "I can be a graphic designer, use my creative talent and capitalize on it." I started to observe daily someone close to me that was a graphic designer. I saw how he mastered the art for his clients, and picked up on his skills. Once I learned how to use the tools correctly, I was again ready to begin focusing on something I was passionate about. I wasn't going into it because someone else wanted it for me; I was going into it because I wanted it for myself.

Here I was, a twenty-one year man, pursuing his passion for art forms while some older, more experienced individuals were still trying to find their passion. It helps to get under the wing of someone who is already where you want to be. This someone must also be willing, and available, to mentor you on success and how to overcome obstacles. Surround yourself with people who are not driven to impress others, but rather driven to leave a legacy for future generations. Being passionate and staying focused is also highly important.

Passion comes from the heart; focus comes from avoiding distractions that may cause you to veer from the path that can take you where you want to be. In order to do this, you must have a reason why you want to make a difference. A reason that is so powerful, it permeates your entire mission. I look back at my past; I came from being a high school dropout to becoming a college student – without first earning a high-school diploma. We cannot accuse anyone for the mistakes we make. We can only learn from them and make corrections.

In high school, I made many mistakes. Because of these mistakes, I eventually dropped out. My mother told me that if I did not get my act together, my friends will go off to college and leave me behind. Her words became my reality. Death and life are in the power of the tongue and those who love it will eat its fruit (Proverbs 18:21). Dropping out of school made me feel like a loser, and I was determined not to fail at anything else.

My mother had also spoken with my football coach and inquired about my progress in school. The news he gave her caused her to burst out in tears. That moment was the game-changer for me. Immediately, I wanted to make a difference and not see my mother cry about things I was doing wrong. I would rather see her cry tears of joy about things I am doing right. After a grueling process, I did earn my diploma, but not before taking college courses.

We often struggle but it is not about how many times you struggle, it's about how many times you get back up with an abundance of unbelievable passion and focus. It was around this time when I began to realize that I owed an obligation to my family to be successful and break the mold. I had to change who I was associated with and what I was doing so that I would be more apt to put things in perspective – *"you will become the equivalent of the five people you spend time with the most."*

## *"Never Allow Your History to Dictate Your Destiny"*

Open your mind and visualize where you want to be. It can be traveling the world, having a great impact on the lives of others, having money left in the bank after all debts are paid, retiring your parents, or earning multiple streams of income. Whatever your vision is, you can pave your way towards the manifestation of it. Being the only entrepreneur in my family, I had to think outside the box. There were times when I even kicked that box to the side.

Just because I made a few mistakes in the past, did not mean my future was any less bright. Much too often, people tend to let what happened in their past keep them from overcoming and accomplishing their dreams. Always remember, our eyes are placed in front of us, because it's more important to look ahead than to look back. Have you ever met someone that could explain how they wanted their future to look and it motivated them to take action? You can do the same thing; you will never know what is waiting ahead of you until you take action to get it.

## *"If You Don't Start TODAY, You Won't Finish TOMORROW"*

Now that you know that your future is awaiting your arrival, you are the only person in to give yourself the green light, GO! It's time to decide that you want to be the person to do something different and stop worrying about where you come from. Look at what's sitting at the top level waiting for you to reach for it. It seems that most successful people have had the toughest past you could ever imagine. But adversity didn't cause them to dim their light of perseverance and veer them off their course of action.

What are you willing to give up today that will make a meaningful change for you tomorrow? Here are a few ways to become the change you need in your life:

**Look Fear In The Face:** I've learned in business that fear does not exist. It's just an emotional response from a bad past experience. Before you get past fear, you must first look it in the face and acknowledge it. I remember as a child going to bed at night with the lights on because I feared something would grab me. I knew eventually I had to face that fear or it would stay with me as I grew older. Today, I have no problem with sleeping in the dark. This same approach to fear applies in life or business; go that extra mile, face your fears, and be determined that fear is not going to delay your progress.

**Motivate Yourself With Fear:** Ren Carlton said it best, *"Fear is a very expensive trait to have. It's a dangerous emotion to deal with and you have to put it aside. If you don't, it will kill you. Inactivity is the worst thing you can do in the business world. You have to be out there mixing it up."* If you want to be the leader of a team, whether it's a business team or a sports team, you must surround around yourself with those who have a reputation for using the mind structure they have. Ask questions, tell them what your fears are, and get advice on how they overcame their obstacles. From that point on, you will be motivated to be held accountable for letting go of the fears that hold you back. After that, the rest is easy.

**Be Coachable and Teachable:** Here is a great nugget from one of my mentors Vincent K. Harris, *"A good friend loves you the way you are, a great mentor loves you too much to leave you the way you are."* Do you see the difference? Mentors have been where you are and have faced the fear you are currently facing. Let them give you all the wisdom and insight you need so that you can utilize their teachings by applying them to your everyday life or in business.

I'm sharing these principles and tips with you because I've learned them along the way doing business with people from different walks of life. When I made the decision to turn my life around, many people laughed at me and thought I was trying to be better than them. Well, that wasn't the case; I was not trying to be better than anyone else but myself. My mind had outgrown my hometown, and I needed to get out and allow things to stretch in my life. I wanted to have and do more for myself, my family, and my loved ones.

I started to notice that there were two things that drive people, those things are, "Desire & Fear." I had to figure out which one was driving me the most; to be honest it felt as though both were equally driving me at the same time. We all experience some type of fear. Fear to move into and beyond what we are called to do and the desire to become what we are destined to be. I had a desire to become a great person and do great things. It was in my heart to reach that mark in my life, I just can't leave this earth and not make a difference. When it's my time to go, I want to say *"Father, I used everything you gave me."* That's what you also have to tell yourself if you really want to achieve something great in life. Push past the obstacles and tell your spirit your family deserves better.

*Chapter 2*

# THE CRASH

*"Empty your mind; be formless, shapeless - like water. Now you put water into a cup, it becomes the cup, you put water into a bottle, it becomes the bottle, you put it in a teapot, and it becomes the teapot. Now water can flow or it can crash. Be water, my friend."*

*– Bruce Lee*

    Staying with my mother and not having the finances to have the freedom I desired, was challenging to say the least. I was sleeping on a fold-up bed that was too small, my clothes were kept in trash bags, and my mind was in conflict between where I was and where I knew I should be. I needed to get my mind off my current situation and decided to take moms' car without her permission to visit a beautiful girl in a city close by. It was a rainy and dreary day, but my spirits were lifted at the thought of seeing her. I dressed with excitement and gathered the car keys from the kitchen counter. My visit with her proved to be a great deterrent for the moment. Driving back from seeing her, I was taking the Burlington exit driving pretty fast and squinting to see through the fog. There was an accident on the freeway that was a hit and run. My heart was pounding in my chest, I was afraid. Being reckless and in a hurry to return the car, I hit someone else driving on the intersecting ramp. The impact was both shocking and a wake-up call.

I had to do the inevitable and call my mother to give her the news that her car was a now a wreck. She was more relieved that I was unharmed, than she was disappointed that her car was totaled. If anything would have happened to me she would have lost her mind. I realized that I was on this earth for a specific purpose, to make mistakes but learn from them so that I may make a difference in the lives of others.

**This chapter outlines:**

- ✓ Overcoming obstacles in life
- ✓ Helping others prevent the crashes of life
- ✓ Being determined to reach and surpass your potential
  *And more!*

Everyone experiences a head on collision at some point in their life, whether it is recklessness, familial disagreements, or not having a father figure. But everyone has someone, somewhere who will love them enough to keep them from crashing and burning. We have a choice to either help people clean their slate and get past the mental and emotional barriers that are holding them back, or sit back and watch them waste their lives away by never leaving a legacy. How could you help someone if you haven't been through any major crashes in your life? Would you really matter to someone if you did?

What are those necessary steps you would take to make sure you left a mark on this earth by making a difference? I truly believe the only person you are destined to *BECOME* is the person you decide to *BE*. Live in such a way so that your character will precede you before you even open your mouth to speak. If life has taught you a lesson, it is now your obligation to teach that lesson to others.

After getting in the car on my way home, I thought about the pain and hurt that I caused my mother. It was because of a bad decision I made, and I felt worthless. I felt like it was a never-ending story that played over-and-over again in my life. As I was looking outside the window of the car, I couldn't see myself doing anything else but finding a solution to my problem. How can I avoid another crash in my life? I am not talking about just a car crash; but a crash that could potentially hurt others. I was determined not to be a statistic; not to let my life go to waste; not to be known as just, *"another one of those guys."*

How will a crash in your life turn into your message? A message that will help better someone else who is going through a lot in their life? What are some things you would do to make an impact on a person's life to help them become better? Do you just hope to make a difference or do you have a vision to be the change you want to see? There's a difference between hope and vision.

Hope is when a person has talent but doesn't apply themselves; vision is when a person takes action because they can see a glimpse of their future. I want this to lie on your heart; when you see someone that has talent, push them to fulfill their dreams and goals in life. Everyone has a dream, but are they in the right environment, and around the right type of people who share their vision and tell them to push harder?

**When You Find Something You Want to Do, GO DO IT!**

Break the Mold

**When You're Steadily Being Blessed With Success, Stay Humble Throughout the Entire Process.**

Break the Mold

**Your Passion Will Take You Places; Walk Into What You Were Called to Do.**

Break the Mold

**You Have What it Takes to Overcome the Crashes in Your Life.**

Break the Mold

**If You're Tired of Starting Over, Stop Giving Up**

Break the Mold

**You Have Every Right to DREAM BIG; Remove Those Who Try to Blind Your Vision.**

Break the Mold

**Never Let Someone Distract You From Achieving Your Goals.**

Break the Mold

*Everyone is not going to like you. But if you're doing the right thing, you have nothing to worry about. Remember, they didn't like Jesus either!*

*Chapter 3*

# THE ENTREPRENEURIAL TURNAROUND

*"We are shifting from a managerial society to an entrepreneurial society."*

*– John Naisbitt*

Now that you have gotten a glimpse of my past, and how I've overcame certain obstacles, now I will share with you how I made the shift towards change.

**The purpose of this chapter:**

- ✓ To help you understand that the words you speak manifests into an existence
- ✓ To show you how to tap into what is right for you
- ✓ How to make a 360° evaluation of your life, and a 180° turnaround; proving that it can be done

I am passionate about empowering others with my story, letting them know that it wasn't easy to break through the most difficult times in my life. But, I made a decision to change. I was inspired by this very thought, *"I will never know whose life I can change until I first change my own."* The thought of making a difference in the lives of others pushed me into action. Sometimes, that's all it takes is a push to create change. Many people do not think before taking action, but it's how well you *THINK* that determines your *LIFESTYLE*.

Has something ever bothered you to the point where you wanted to do something about it? It could be helping someone you care about move out of a bad neighborhood. Or it could be a stranger on the street freezing with no home, asking for "change" so he can get a meal. If it bothers you, chances are it is your purpose to extend yourself for the sake of others, and end the crash in their lives. By opening yourself up as a servant to others, you may even help steer someone in the right direction that you didn't even know was hurting.

It is never too late to make a significant turnaround. But before your life spirals too far out of control, you must be willing to remove yourself out of the equation and take the task of, "breaking the mold," more seriously. *The best way to accept change is to let it GROW on you.* For months while in school, I was out with friends – being unproductive and wasting my time and talent. It finally dawned on me: I needed to take the time that is required to develop a skill I was already good at, and extremely passionate about. . I needed to grow into my change

I received a letter that tuition had gone up tremendously at the university I was attending. My mom and I couldn't afford to pay any additional expenses, so I went back home to figure something out. I learned from one of my mentors that, *"Every problem has a solution."* I remembered that statement and was determined not to give up. I went home disappointed because I was right back at my starting point. I knew I had to get a job and help out around the house. I began working in manufacturing companies operating machines, but was unfulfilled. After working those types of jobs for months up to a few years, I realized that my talent was being wasted.

## *"Whatever Lives in Your MOUTH, Lives in Your FUTURE"*

Going through life I've learned a lot, but I realized that knowledge is only the beginning. I must also apply the knowledge. When I'm around certain people, I ask myself why do they complain so much and speak negatively all the time. As I continued to grow and my mindset began to change, I promised myself that whatever it takes I will speak positive words and speak wisely. I apply that knowledge daily. The words we speak are very powerful, they either can create life or death. For example, just as you plant a seed in the ground to grow, as long as it has water it grows - "that's life." But if you stop watering the flowers, eventually they begin to die - "that's death."

It gets difficult when feelings get in the way and your mouth wants to speak what your heart feels. But with a tough mind and applied wisdom, we can avoid those negative thoughts and keep pressing. I stayed around my mentors often to make sure I learned what I knew I needed to know, I learned a lot by doing that. Mentors are people who see your potential, and guide on how to reach your goals. If you have a successful mentor and they sincerely believe in you, then there's something about you that they like.

Most of them will not waste their time on someone without any potential; they will just keep leading in the process. However, everything happens in due season just as the bible states in Galatians 6:9, *"Let us not become weary in doing good, for at the proper time you will reap a harvest if you do not give up.*" If you do not have a mentor who will invest their time with you, it is your responsibility to strengthen your potential and seek one out. Once you have one, you do not need to like everything about them, but be grateful for them and respect them as a business person. Great example, I've worked many jobs in my past that I did not like but I was grateful to have one because it allowed me to pay bills, have money in the bank, and invest in my future.

Other people may complain and speak negatively about their situation or about the job that they asked for, signed the application for, and interviewed for. They may not realize they are speaking things into their life and it causes them to become even more frustrated. I remained mentally focused by not complaining, learning from others, making sure I got the job done, and doing what I needed to do - *That's how you overcome*. I knew deep down in my heart I would reap a harvest and get promoted to that next season in my life. Our brain operates off the words we speak and the images we hold in our minds. Therefore, when you can speak what you see, eventually you'll see what you spoke.

If the people in your inner circle are not speaking powerful words into your life and you're not seeing significant change, then it's time to find a new circle of people. In the beginning of my growing stages, I started to realize what we think about manifests into our lives. It can either be beneficial to our purpose, or it can become another piece of baggage that holds you back from grasping what you really want out of life. Throughout the years, I have followed the teachings of and listened to so many leaders who have power and influence such as Dr. Myles Munroe Bishop T.D. Jakes, John C. Maxwell, Dr. Stephen R. Covey, Anthony

"Tony" Robbins, and many more. The things they speak about continue to inspire me to become a better person, using everything I have in me so that I "DON'T WASTE TALENT."

## *"Live With Enthusiasm. Whatever You Do, Give it Your Best"*

I have stated this many times during conversations, I usually end up explaining what I mean by it. When I expand on that statement and add something like, entrepreneurs thrive on having a lifelong vision and aspire to create the future, not only for themselves but for the world. The other discussion comes after they ask, "How can you possibly be the best in the world?" But that isn't what I meant, I would say these words, "Give it your best" meaning stay in your lane and be the best, and do everything in your power to give your all. Why would a person want to live a mediocre life and not walk in the purpose they were created to fulfill? *"Knowledge is power and enthusiasm pulls the switch"* that made all the sense in the world when Steve Droke stated this.

Since leaving my job, a job that wasn't for me, I immediately turned on the switch and make a significant change. It was time to get things done, have fun, gain more clients, attract more like-minded individuals, and attain better communication skills. It takes a lot of energy to be enthusiastic, so if you're experiencing difficulty feeling that drive, then it might be because you need to make a change and create your own turnaround.

## "Chase Your Dreams, Don't Stay Stuck in Your Comfort Zone"

There are 3 types of people, and I run across them every day. These people are those who follow their dreams, those who do nothing, and those who chase their dreams at full speed on a much higher level. I remember riding in the car with one of my mentors one day, we were conversing and I asked him what inspired him to go after his dreams. He stated, one of his own mentors told him, "don't wait until you get in your 30's and 40's and realize that you haven't accomplished anything and you're still broke." That inspired me to start chasing my dreams at full speed, rather than merely following them.

Have you ever really analyzed how you have spent most of your time? When we stretch our minds to new dimensions and expand our territories, we often realize we could have done more. Don't get so caught up in your comfort zone that you forget about what really matters, it's time to hit that switch and make a complete turn. Become the entrepreneur you really want to be. When life gets tough, get tougher and turn your story around. Here's the thing, what's really great about this is that you don't need to fit into the 3 types of people – you can think outside the box.

There are millions of people who have all the potential in the world to make a complete turnaround in their lives and to help improve the lives of others. Everyone has the chance to be a person who strives for growth and self-discovery - never stay inside a predetermined box. I will discuss this topic more in a later chapter. Make opportunities for yourself; seek out what really matters to you. Help others find their dreams and make them a reality. Jim Rohn, made one of the best statements of all time, he stated *"You will have anything you WANT in life if you will help other people get what they WANT."*

## Chapter 4

# GET YOUR DREAM BACK

*"Go confidently in the direction of your dreams. Live the life you have imagined."*

*– Henry David Thoreau*

If you have lost sight of your goals for each week, month and year and can't regain focus, you will have to get back into position so that you can be ahead of your game. If you can't find time to make it work, this chapter is for you.

**What you will learn:**

- ✓ Understanding your purpose and staying consistent in it.
- ✓ Taking control of your day and blocking negative thoughts.
- ✓ How to put your business first while impacting lives.

As an entrepreneur, there will be a point where you will feel like no one supports your vision or believes in you. Although you may have what it takes to be successful, the skills and correct mindset; there may be times when you feel incomplete. Times you will feel you are missing a piece that is needed to complete your puzzle. That missing piece may be your father, brother, sister, mother, mentor or perhaps a good friend. Some of those people you may have to leave behind during the start of your journey, you can always reach out to them later.

Positive people who support you will be there with you every step of the way. But those who are negative and only around for what they can gain from you will only be with you for a moment. To avoid being sucked into negativity, you must have unbelievable focus, undeniable passion, and great mental toughness. The good thing about this is that you don't have to have everything in place at one once; all you have to do is pin-point what's right for you and make an educated decision based on how you see your life unfolding. That dream is inside you, all you need to do is get your dream back and push through.

One of the reasons we experience adversity is so that we may become wiser than we were before. Here are a few dynamic quotes that will give you the push you need:

## *"Remind Yourself Daily That You Have What it Takes"*

Once you internalize this and start believing in yourself, the universe will get out of your way. If you are the only entrepreneur in your family or circle of friends, wouldn't you want to break the mold, show them it can and should be done, break the cycle, and be the one who makes a difference? It takes a person of great determination and a million-dollar mindset to take massive action. To get back the dream that was lost due to people telling you that you couldn't achieve it (simply because they wouldn't be able to), it is imperative to make a habit of reminding yourself of what's important to you. These are the things we tend to lack because of the dark clouds in our mind at times.

**Listed here are a few reminders to help you on this journey:**

**You are human:** This is possibly the biggest reminder of them all. You will become your own worst enemy if there's no structure in place for your life. You must have written goals and a structure to accomplish your dreams. There will be bumps along the way, and you will stumble. You may not like where this road will take you at times. But be grateful that you're not where you used to be and understand that you're still an imperfect human being.

**You are in control of your own destiny:** You can't completely predict which turns life will take, or how things will ultimately go. However, you can control the choices you make because your choices will determine how you live your life.

**You have to find a hiding place away from the world:** Sometimes you need to go into your hiding place, away from constantly being the radar of the world. This allows you to regain focus on getting your dreams back in order. Cluttered minds cannot function well, but if you're still, your mind conjures up and brings your dreams to fruition.

**Never, ever, ever, give up:** When you're close to what you're about to achieve, don't give up, go further. Keep going until you reach your mark, and check-off that goal.

## *"Your Reason WHY Should Be So POWERFUL, it Changes You From Who You Used to BE"*

What do you think you were put on this earth to do? Whose life do you want to change for the better? What is your legacy? I ask these questions because once we are able to identify our purpose in life; we can then lead ourselves to our true destiny. One of my mentors once told me, "Your destiny is attached to someone else's." In other words, during the journey to your destiny, you must help someone else get to their own destiny along the way. You must have at least one strong reason why you want to make a difference, and it should be able to spark determination in you every time you think of it. Keep this in mind and it will inspire you to lay out your game plan and take action towards accomplishing your goals.

My reason *why* is my family and the legacy I will leave to future generations, including the children I have yet to be blessed with and their children. Although I went to college without a high school diploma, the dean emphasized that I must have my diploma before the semester ended in order to continue college. Well, I made the decision to move forward, and with my dedication and determination, I earned my diploma and walked the stage with a proud look on my face. I was not the only one who was proud of this achievement, my family was proud of me as well. The look on their faces seeing me walk that stage was priceless - It was like an inauguration of greater things to come, the first step to breaking many molds.

## *"On the Road to SUCCESS, You Will Make Many Mistakes"*

The most common mistake people make is to make the same mistake multiple times. The definition of insanity is doing the same thing over and over again and expecting different results. We should be able to learn from our mistakes, gain wisdom from them, and allow ourselves not t make the same mistakes over and over. Even leaders make mistakes, but a great leader learns from each one. The same thing applies to certain people in your life who may have wronged you; get past the things you perceive they have done to you. Stop trying to get revenge; and start working on what you're passionate about.

Do you pay attention to how you spend your time? Since getting my dream back, I learned how to manage my time much more wisely and staying focused. It is a huge disservice to you if you are scattered between ideas and putting your energy into all of them at once. You won't get anywhere fast doing that. Getting what's rightfully yours requires logical thinking, good timing, and unwavering focus. If you find yourself thinking heavily about vacations, watching television, being on social media just to socialize every hour on the hour, your business plan, and family issues - how can you stay focused, dedicated, and determined to make your dream a reality?

Every morning some people pray before getting up, some people don't pray they just get up and get their day started. I'm not perfect, so there were many days where I would get up and forget to pray. But most of the time I pray before getting my day started. Your purpose is who you are, not what you do. What you do could be your talents, but who you are is what's in your heart, and what you desire. No one can take away what you have been called to do but YOU. Knowing what you are called to do and being consistent in bringing it to fruition is important - eventually you will begin to see results.

I was taught by one of my mentors to jot down affirmations and read them aloud while brushing my teeth. If you do this daily, you will start to see a dramatic change in your life. It has been proven that if you write down the things that you want in your life, they will have a much higher chance of materializing. You will find samples of daily affirmations in the final chapter of this book. Take control of your day by speaking into the atmosphere, and attract into your life anything you desire.

When you truly believe in something the universe will move out of the way, allowing it to materialize. This is how your brain works: you speak aloud what it is you want, it listens and immediately starts working towards making it happen for you. Whatever you focus on, you attract, and it will show up for you because you spoke it into existence. But you must be careful what you focus on, simply saying aloud the opposite of what you want will attract what you don't want. For example, if you want to be a millionaire, say "I am a millionaire." Never say, "I am broke."

Doing so will attract poverty into your life. This is where you will need the mental toughness I spoke of earlier. You must block out what's causing you to steer in the opposite direction from where you want to be. If you follow these simple steps every day, you will experience a shift in your life. Be consistent when creating change in your life.

Consistency to purpose requires focus. Therefore, you want to focus on your primary goals and take decisive, immediate action. Create and pursue goals that are set up for you to win. What I mean by this is, do not set goals that are too big. For example, instead of setting a goal to learn 3 new languages within a year; set a goal to immerse yourself in social settings with people who speak one language you want to learn. If you do this consistently, you will learn to speak the language naturally.

During this transformation process, become a person who is productive but never too busy to appreciate your journey and change the blueprint of it if you must. Many people try to aim for perfection when reaching towards their goals, but excellence (not perfection) is the key to getting things accomplished. Spend time with the people who are already where you want to be professionally and/or personally. This will help you to create a balance in your life so that you will be able to motivate and inspire others while inspiring and motivating yourself.

*Chapter 5*

# IDEAS NEED LEADERS

From the last chapter were you able to see yourself so far into the future that it made you want to push and take action towards it? The idea is to separate the old you of your past by creating a brand new you worthy of the future you desire. Imagine how good it is going to feel when you're no longer where you used to be. You're either a leader, or you are becoming a leader. Wherever you are in your journey, the ideas inside the dark room of your mind needs a leader to develop.

Your ideas need someone who will lead them to influence those who will also take lead. It turns out that most entrepreneurs who are serious about success can visualize their ideas but some of them don't write them down. Therefore, they will sometimes lose an idea that could change their lives and the lives of others. There is power in a dedicated person who sees their vision and writes it down.

**This chapter covers:**

- ✓ Overcoming mental wars and challenges
- ✓ Taking full responsibility and capitalizing on your ideas
- ✓ The role of a powerful servant leader

## Key Principle #1
### *"Our BIGGEST Battles Are Never Physical, They're MENTAL"*

Mental motivation is something that comes from within, and separates the highly successful entrepreneur from the merely good one. It separates the person who only wishes, and the person who takes action. A person without mental motivation can have all the natural talents or abilities and not make it as far as someone with average ability. Ideas and so-called leaders come a dime a dozen. What separates those who are true leaders from the rest is the ability to turn an idea into a legacy, who has a desire to change the lives of others, and who believes in their own future.

Winning in the business world is a mental process, a war if you will. One has to be mentally fit when developing strategies to win the battle. History tells us that significant mental power has shaped the future of people, organizations, and even nations. Look at great leaders such as *Bill Gates, Steve Jobs, Oprah Winfrey, Michael Jordan, and Martin Luther King Jr.* and how they stuck with an idea with purpose in mind. None of them allowed any challenges or distractions to get them off track; they transformed nations and changed the world.

## Key Principle #2
### *"S.M.A.R.T. Success Means Achieving Results Together"*

Have you ever taken on a role but knew there was no way possible that you could do everything without help? John

Boyd said it best, *"People, Ideas, and Technology"* in that order. He was stating that professional leadership is contingent upon the core set of ideas concerning who we are, where we are headed, and the set of values and principles that guide our journey. Collectively this forms a leadership philosophy expressed in our choices, actions, and behavior.

When making smart business decisions, having a team to help lead an idea will bring more value. Why do I say that? When there's a solid foundation to build on, your team will bring thoughts and ideas to the company that perhaps you may not have thought of. As a result, everyone contributes to the expansion of the company yet have full responsibility over their own actions.

## Key Principle #3
*"Always Do Your Best. What You Plant Now, Will HARVEST Later"*

Augustine "Og" Mandino was right on the money when stating this. Difficult times will come, but remember there is something waiting for you that is for you. Go for it and remember your legacy depends on what you do today. The world operates on principles and actions, and if a thought or idea is not acted on immediately, it has a greater chance of disappearing. I find it difficult to understand how most individuals have a vision for their lives, yet won't take action on it quickly.

Just think for a second, what if you were the one person who thought of an idea acted on it immediately and it changed the history of future generations? How good would that make you feel? What if acting on that idea changed your current situation and you didn't have to work a traditional job for the rest of your life? The point I'm making here is that you must take action on what you believe in, even if you fail. I learned this from my mentor Vincent K. Harris, *"You can't expect to reap a harvest in something you haven't sown into."*

## Key Principle #4
*"The Mind is Like a Paintbrush, it Can Color Any Situation"*

Your thoughts are influenced by the books you read and the people who you associate with, but it does not always happen in a direct manner. Sometimes, people can be vicariously influenced by the teachings, actions, and/or mistakes of others. Allow the mind to absorb experiences and use those experiences to paint the picture for your life. If you surround yourself with negativity, you will learn negative habits. Consider the cliché "food for thought," what you feed your mind can either give clarity or be a hindrance to your future. Gary Coxe said, "Never allow someone to rent space in your head," let me add, "If they aren't influencing you to be and do more." It's time to be around some different people.

The mind is so powerful that if you master what you don't know by taking time to study them, you can go on to teach them to your team and organizations; doing this will bring about productive change. It starts with removing the mental clutter, not having anything around you that's distracting, and having discipline that allows you to focus on a certain tasks. An impaired mind cannot paint a promising future.

**An impaired mind brainwashes you to believe:**

- ✓ You can't accomplish anything, allowing you to believe what others think about you
- ✓ You can't think for yourself
- ✓ You are lacking on goals and desires
- ✓ You do not need to follow your daily affirmation agenda along with taking action
- ✓ You don't have to take the important steps to better your future

Once you decide that enough is enough, it is then time to get refocused. A business is the reflection of its owner and how it is operated. You will want to replace your impaired thinking with thoughts of success and prosperity.

**Say to yourself:**

- ✓ I have what it takes to be successful
- ✓ I stay away from people who slow up my process
- ✓ I am around power people who can shorten my learning curve
- ✓ I will have a set schedule for my future and I am sticking to it
- ✓ I have balance in my life
- ✓ I am focused on personal growth for the next level in life and business
- ✓ *Now take action!*

# Key Principle #5
*"When You Focus on TODAY, You Will Be Ready for a Great TOMORROW"*

I've learned in my years of business and in life that although tomorrow is not here yet, when we focus on what needs to take place today, we will be better off tomorrow. Many people get anxious about tomorrow and get taken away from the priorities that need to be completed today. When you're disciplined and determined to do what it takes today, you will be well prepared and not bombarded with things that come your way tomorrow. If you read the scripture (Matthew 6:34) it states, *"Do not worry about tomorrow, for tomorrow will care for itself."* Some people are more prone to worry than others, but worrying is a waste of time and can be prevented.

## Key Principle #6
*"As We Are THINKING and SPEAKING, We Are CREATING"*

If you don't understand this principle in life and business, you will continue to welcome failure by attracting into your life the things you do not want. Have you ever said you need a job and it doesn't matter what job you take? A couple of days or a few months later, you get a call for a position and everything sounds okay during the interview process. However, when you start the new position you realize it's not something you like or you're passionate about. Remember, you must be specific when you want something manifested into your life.

Many people don't take the time to actually describe what they want; they allow their emotions to drive them and they end up in situations they don't like. Working on something you don't like means you're simply wasting talent. Use wisdom and with an expanded mindset, you'll know exactly what you want. You will want to start a business doing something that ignites your passion and drive. Your words should be described like this:

- ✓ I want to start a business working for myself, but I need to get a job that I'm passionate about to fund my dreams.
- ✓ I have created a written plan to map out my future success and will present it to investors who are liable
- ✓ Lord, enlarge my territory and bring the right people into my life that see my vision
- ✓ I am winning in the race of life
- ✓ I will prosper and become wealthy as my business takes off so that I may better help others

## Key Principle #7
*"You Never Know Whose Life You Will Change, Until You First Change Your Own"*

Change comes from within; no one can change a person but themselves. When I started hanging around different people who had the same desires and mindset that I had, my mindset started to expand. I eventually outgrew where I came from because I wanted more out of life. Ideas began to pop up in my mind, and as they were popping I started writing them down. I did that so when I wanted to start working on that particular idea, I could refer back to that piece of paper. I changed for the best because I knew I wanted more for my family.

Learning was a process and I always knew that if I focused on an "amount" it would be for just that moment, however when focusing on an "idea" it was for a LIFETIME.

Never become so comfortable with yourself that you forget that the ideas you have can possibly change everything else around you. But you first have to want to change yourself - how can a person change the world and never change himself? It isn't possible. Change is always a good thing; you just have to want it for yourself and everyone else as well. *"You are one thought away from changing the lives of your family,"* this is how great leaders think in order to create generational wealth.

## Key Principle #8
"Every Business Has the Potential to Become a Great Enterprise."

Do you want to have a great enterprise? If you want to know where you'll be in 5 to 10 years from now, just listen to what you talk about the most - *"Your tongue is a rudder."* What if I was to present you with a step-by-step plan on how to build a great enterprise as tried and proven to work by many successful entrepreneurs, would you be willing to learn? Since we are embarking on that next step, I want to clearly state that all you have to have is a dream, a strong back bone, a plan to build something great, along with dedication, and determination. After studying and learning the secrets on how Oprah Winfrey, Henry Ford, Aliko Dangote, Bill Gates, John D. Rockefeller, Mark Zuckerberg, J. Paul Getty, and Mark Cuban became so successful, I realized it really wasn't a "secret" at all.

In fact, most of them are school dropout billionaires. Proving that all you need is the will to make good decisions, have dedication, and determination. I'm a fan and owner of many personal development and business books. In the book "Make Today Count," John Maxwell highlighted, *"the secret to your success is determined by your daily agenda."* That is so true. Let that sink into your spirit for a moment.

Throughout our lives, we meet people who over exaggerate yesterday, overestimate tomorrow, and underestimate today. In today's world, we tend to focus on the economy too much, complain often about yesterday, what we should have done, and the things that did not go right. Then we tend to have these big plans of what we will do tomorrow, but the fact is we forget about the importance of today. Whatever it is you do, don't allow your ideas to go to waste, stand firm as a bona fide leader on what you believe in.

## Chapter 6
# THE DANGER OF GIVING UP TOO SOON

*"When You Feel Like Giving Up, Remember Why You Held On For So Long in the First Place"*

*— Unknown*

Many people give up, and others realize that if they give up on something, they will never see it in their future. A lot of times you have to see the big picture, move beyond what you thought you were capable of doing – that's how you grow. Always remember this philosophy, *"If you don't have rain in your life, you can't GROW."* This statement is very true and applies to everyday life situations whether it's business, personal, or financially related. Things don't always come easy, but when you make good decisions, are dedicated to your goals, and determined to win, you won't give up easily.

As a leader you have to take full accountability for what you do because there are people in your circle who are counting on you and watching your every move. It helps to be the passenger sometimes, stop taking the wheel all the time. You have to allow God to drive your way through so life doesn't cause you to have any self-doubt. Free your mind from the poverty mindset, and create an abundance mindset.

Many people blame the recession for their financial problems, but the only recession is how your mind thinks. You can master anything once your mind has mastered the thought of overcoming.

In this chapter I will share a few things with you to help you understand that even if you give up on your process today, you will still be held accountable for the following:

- ✓ Legacy Motivation
- ✓ How many lives you could possibly change
- ✓ Changing your family's history and future generations
- ✓ Giving Back
- ✓ Fulfilling God's purpose
- ✓ Leading someone else to their destiny
- ✓ Helping others avoid mistakes

Some of these things may not be what you want to do; maybe they are irrelevant to you. But if you are reading this book, you are a leader and you will either lead others to their success or their devastation. The choice is yours. Just think, for every check point above you can change someone else's life and your own in the process. Here's how:

- ✓ Inspiring your family and making a significant change to take them to new levels in life
- ✓ Change lives and help solve people's problems. That way, you aren't only helping yourself but helping change the lives of others
- ✓ Provide those who are in need, and make a difference in your community

- ✓ You might have a purpose of your own, but in fulfilling God's purpose you will be rewarded
- ✓ Help others shorten their learning curve
- ✓ People will make mistakes, but you can help them not make the same mistake twice

Did you know that life gives you a test? The test is to see how you can handle certain situations, either they make you stronger or make you throw in the towel. The key is to figure out what's important to you and make it work. If your plan doesn't work, come up with a different strategy, or seek the advice of mentors who have already been where you want to go. Mentors are just like road maps; they are designed to teach and guide you through certain areas in life.

You only have three choices in life: Give up, give in, or give it all you've got. It is important that you *JUST DON"T GIVE UP TOO SOON.* Is it a normal reaction to choose to give up? Is it commendable to be moved by what you feel instead of what you believe? Is it acceptable to quit pursuing your goals? The answer to all these questions is a big NO!

## Top 7 Reasons You Should NEVER Give Up

**Your Family and Friends:** Make a decision to put every effort into focusing on your dreams. There's at least one person in your family who is counting on you to make a difference.

**Your Legacy:** What is your legacy? What is something so great and important that you want to leave it to your children and their children? Dedicate time to creating your legacy; doing this is more important than giving up.

**Happiness:** Every time you have the urge or feel the need to give up, start to send a positive signal to your mind telling it that it can accomplish anything. Change your thinking.

**There Are People Worse-Off:** Look at your life right now and look at someone else's life that has it worse than you. Right now someone is wishing they could have what you have.

**You Are Too Close:** Look at how far you've come. You have been provided with everything you need to fulfill your destiny. Stop making excuses and just make it happen.

**You Deserve the Best:** Don't settle for less, settling is telling your spirit that you don't deserve better. When you do this you are lowering your standards.

**Talent Is Your Gift Back to God:** I love this quote by Leo Buscaglia, *"Your talent is God's gift to you, what you do with it is your gift back to God."* I've often heard that if you don't use your gifts and talents, they will be taken away from you. I refuse to know personally if that is true, I'm using my gifts and talents. Are you?

What does it take to overcome from giving up too soon? The answer is what makes Breaking the Mold so special, is that it takes a change in your mindset and a means to do just that. Nine years ago, I chose to go a different route rather than follow the crowd. I said to myself if my THINKING changes, my LIFE will change for the better. You have an obligation to fulfill your purpose because your dreams have been planted into your heart by the Creator. If you do not fulfill these dreams, a burden will settle on your heart and you will start to feel guilty.

This seems to be a pattern within our society, people tend to give up on their dreams not because they don't have what it takes, but because of the people they spend time with. Well, I'm here to tell you to put your dreams and goals back in your heart because one day you will wake up and there won't be any more time to do the things you've always wanted. The key to success is persistence; the only thing that is stopping you is yourself.

I've had the opportunity to listen to other people's stories for years and I'm sure you have too. The most common thing I hear is that some of the people they care about don't support their dreams, which causes them to get frustrated and lose sight of what they want to accomplish. I went through the same situation I remember my friends used to laugh and joke about what I wanted to do, but I didn't let that stop me. I rose above the ridicule, and was determined to succeed because I believed in myself - That is something you have to do as well. Here's a quote I live by day-to-day, *"Success is not an option, it's a MANDATORY MEETING."*

Let me paint the picture for you so that you can see it within your mind, let's say you're on your job and the manager or supervisors call for a mandatory meeting for all employees. Key word "Mandatory" which means you must be there; if you miss this mandatory meeting you could be penalized or possibly lose your job. It's the same way with success in your life and business. But you have to be willing to make progress. And the major part about making progress is the *MENTAL* side. Here's another statement of mine that I would like to share:

*"I've failed a lot in my life, but the thought of giving up never existed. You have to keep your mind leveled to where it's mentally focused and away from all the distractions, mental*

*clutter, disappointments, hurt, depression, and discouragement. Always remember, **"Our greatest battles are not physical, they're MENTAL."***

I believe the same principle was used with successful name brands. Just think to yourself how major corporations and individuals stuck with what they believed in. They built a team of already motivated individuals who believed in "ONE VISION, ONE BRAND, ONE COMPANY," which inspired them to go further and find every solution to any problems that surely came about. I've been guilty of giving up too soon in life but the one thing that kept me from being bombarded and straying away from what was important, was not allowing my mind to be cluttered. Family, friends, things, objects, and even colleagues will discourage you from going after what you really want in life.

If you don't have something to look forward to, such as bold dreams and a big future, then your soul isn't being nourished. Les Brown stated, *"You've Got to Be Hungry."* You have to take responsibility and develop a hunger for success to achieve your dreams. What do you do when you're hungry? You EAT. It's the same way with success, if you get hungry for it – you will find a way to have it.

## *"It Doesn't Matter Where You've Been, It Only Matters Where You're Headed"*

The key in life is to keep looking towards your future, however if you don't take action, you will continue to stay in the same place. Most people say, "I have a bright future" but then they sit on their butt and hardly ever apply themselves in life to become a better person, to go from "Good to Great".

It's imperative to commit yourself to lifelong learning. The greatest asset in life is the peace of mind of knowing what you have, what you want to accomplish, and having a circle of supporters who are loyal and trustworthy. Just picture in your mind, if you were to give up today; what would things look like for you in the future?

In today's world, people no longer value persistence, preparation, dedication, and determination. When one stumbling block comes our way, we often want to give up and not carry on with the process. Sometimes teenagers will quit school just 8 weeks before graduation, when in all honesty they could have made it if they would have kept focused just a little while longer. My story was slightly different; I didn't drop out because I *wanted* to give up. Dropping out was the result of my poor choices. But because of these choices, I ended up giving up on myself too soon.

I'm sure you get the picture. Giving up is never an option for a long-term outcomes. Take for instance, Michael Jordan's' story, when he got cut from his high school basketball team. Of course he was heartbroken and devastated. But after that, he was determined to create his own future, he simply went in his backyard and mastered the game of basketball. Now today, look at his "BRAND" and legacy he's leaving for his children and future generations. He went from adversity to overcoming, and breaking the mold. What if MJ decided to just give up and work at traditional job? This same motivation applies to you, never give up too soon.

*Chapter 7*

# EXECUTION IS AN ART

Thanks for turning over to this chapter; I hope you learned something from the last chapter and understand that you can't give up too soon. You can't afford to waste talent, you must learn to execute your ideas because time waits for no one. Execution can be quite difficult and draining at times, but you must not take, "NO" for an answer, and never make excuses as to why can't accomplish your goals. People's visions often die because of the lack of taking action on them, funding, and lack of knowledge as to what to do and where to start. What's the hold up on your execution?

In many ways, people come up with different ways to circumvent their thoughts and skilled talents; they find every possible way to think of why they can't do something instead of figuring out a solution to do it. It's simple really, *"Don't let what you CAN'T do, prevent you from what you CAN do."* Once you switch your thinking, everything else starts to find its way towards you. However you MUST make the decision to execute.

If working in the corporate sector isn't for you, at least stretch your mind to having a corporate mindset. It doesn't matter if you are in the urban field, a gospel artist, a college student, etc.; I believe entrepreneurship is about starting somewhere. It can, it does, and it should start at a young age. What we learn early stays with us for life.

**Here are some mistakes young entrepreneurs tend to make:**

- ✓ Acting on their emotions and not consulting with someone who's specialized in that particular practice or in that specific field
- ✓ Not realizing that business is business and personal is personal, allowing their emotions to kick in and keep them from letting others to help them
- ✓ Not having a mentor that's in the same field or realm of business
- ✓ Making money and not using portions to fund back into their projects
- ✓ Not implementing dynamic strategies and planning properly
- ✓ Wasting time and resources

**Here are some steps you should take and get ready to execute:**

- ✓ Sit down with a mentor who has the same mindset and/or has studied the industry that you're in
- ✓ Build a team or get in a quiet area to lay out a detailed game plan for your product or business you're aiming to launch
- ✓ Implement different strategies and don't worry about the funds, they will come
- ✓ Don't let your emotions take over your passion
- ✓ Start the process

Everyone is unique in their own way of doing things. But it's the common little things that count, and which reflects the amount of effort you put into your dreams. What works for others simply doesn't work for everyone else. I'm going to share how I execute strategies and ideas on a daily basis and how I get through them mentally. Remember, we stop ourselves from achieving things because we get in our own way.

Going back to chapter 4, "Get Your Dream Back," I spoke about getting up and reading my daily affirmations. Firstly, when I wake up I have to give God prayer and thank Him. I've learned to never wake up without thanking God for everything He has done. Secondly, I often find that reading my affirmations and speaking them into the atmosphere 5 times a day, I tend to draw more of a passionate force. That force drives me to get things accomplished because my mind operates off of what I speak.

## *"Anyone Can Steal Ideas, But No One Can Steal EXECUTION or PASSION"*

I'm sure you've heard it before "execution and passion goes hand in hand," it's true – you can't have one with the other. Here's what I mean by that. You need to have the willpower to execute something based on a thought, you need the passion to go out and make it happen. It is empowering to be able to step-out of your comfort zone and do something different than from what everyone else is doing. Did you know that you aren't just powerful, but you are POWER itself? You are more than capable of making things happen. Most individuals fall short of seeking personal development in order to learn new skills, and to weigh the pros and cons of their execution. They aren't motivated to bring to life what they really want to do. Some who do may start off small, and others start off with the process of doing things on a larger scale because they have done their research. It's okay to be unique in your execution because the way you execute is unlike anyone else. The person who said, "be yourself, every else is taken," was exactly right.

Over the years of doing business, I've learned these 5 critical components that every individual or company needs:

1. **Business Plan**
   A well-written business plan includes a good marketing plan and knowing your target audience. The most common mistake made is when a person doesn't do their research, if you don't know anything about a business plan, do your research first and hire someone, write the plan yourself, or hire someone to review the plan you wrote in detail. *"People who fail to plan, plan to fail."*

2. **Money**
   Your dreams don't stop just because you might not have the money. If you're working a job, make sure you put monies to the side to start your own business. Remember, your business is a reflection of yourself. Most cases you have to be in business for two years in order to get a loan from the bank. However, do not skip step 1, you will need a business plan to present to them.

3. **Website, Logo & Marketing Materials**
   The beginning stages of growing your business, you must have a brand that catches the eye of your target

audience; if it doesn't, you lose. Marketing your business and building a brand name is not just for big companies, it starts with you as an individual. Branding your business is important as growing your company, big or small. Repetition, consistency, and visibility are the keys to building a successful brand. Below are branding materials you will need.

**Branding:** A brand can be defined as, "a name, logo, slogan, and/or design scheme associated with a product or service." If you are in business today, it's imperative that you brand your business with a first-rate logo, website, business cards, letterhead, print ads, etc. You can breakdown simple key elements to branding your business.

A. **Logo:** A logo should be effective, an eye opener, and able to brand you and what you're doing. It affects your business just as a person is the reflection of their company. Just look at some of the big name brands such as: Verizon, Sprint, Dell, Apple, Microsoft, and many more. They all have one thing in common *"simplicity."*

B. **Website:** Many people say your website is your online presence, but in many cases it's also your online business card. Having your logo presented on every page of your website shows that your company is consistent. Have you ever seen websites out there that look too busy? That means it was too much thought put into it, when all they had to do was make it look clean and professional. Once you have a clean professional look, then it's time to promote.

C. **Business Cards:** Business Cards are your tools to approach other professionals and introduce yourself. Make sure your logo is displayed properly, and your card includes your contact information and your companies address. If you work from home, never include your home address. Your first impression is your last impression.

D. **Letterhead:** Letterheads are for all purpose business, be sure to include your logo, company information and contact information. You have to be mindful that all of your branding should coordinate with one another with consistency.

4. **Strategies for Social Networks:** Many people are using social networking sites, even big brand name companies because they know the importance and they are FREE! Why not utilize them?

Most social networking sites can be used to target a specific audience that you cater to, make sure you know where your audience is located. Create strategic plans to promote yourself, a product, or service. If you look at the major people who are making money, impacting lives, inspiring individuals, and providing good content, they are building relationships. Nurturing relationships is the key to build your business and marketing your brand.

*"There are Two Things That Doesn't Work Well When They're Closed: A Parachute and a CLOSED MIND"*

Use your imagination here for a moment; first imagine yourself getting off a plane. You're about to skydive. You are wearing a parachute and you jump off - can you feel the intensity? Now imagine the parachute not opening, it remains closed, what are you going to do now? Picture in your mind the same thing but you jump off and the parachute opens, you feel much better because you can guide your own way through the air.

It's the same thing with an open mind and a closed mind, when you have an open mind you can guide yourself in such a way that you attract opportunities to you. Having an open mind really works, but when your mind is closed you prevent opportunities from coming your way. It means you're preventing yourself from achieving the most out of life. Why would a person do such a thing? Keep your mind open to new possibilities because there's so much more that this world has to offer and it's a terrible thing to waste talent. Books, being around the right people, and the words you speak allow your mind to stretch open.

### *"A Good Attitude Will Open More Doors Than Your Talent Will"*

The one thing I tell my mentees is that people don't buy products and services, they buy PEOPLE. Once you understand this concept, then you'll know exactly how it works. Mark Twain said it best, "people only do business with who they KNOW, LIKE & TRUST," if you're in business, it just makes sense. Believe it or not, everyone is not going to like you, some people are not going to do business with you for multiple reasons. But you cannot dwell on them, move on to the next person or opportunity.

Hiring someone for their services alone or buying their products is not why people tend to do business with them. It's the fact that they know, like, or trust them; which is crucial in expanding your business. Some people think they can attend events, mingle in the community, shake a few hands, pass out a business card or two, and everything flows well - in most cases, it takes a little bit more effort than that. You never know who is watching and testing you to see how well you build networks and relationships. Once people know, like, and trust you, they will want to do business with you.

I was at networking event when I witnessed three gentlemen who came in from another city two of which who had no clue what networking was all about. The first gentleman approached me and introduced himself. He gave me a short speech about what he did then proceeded to go to the next person. The second one shook my hand, handed me his promotional materials, and didn't bother to give his name. But the last one introduced himself, shook my hand, had the correct posture, and started an ordinary conversation.
Instead of giving a spiel about himself, he asked me what I do professionally. Now, that is how you build relationships. I would do business with this man, because he obviously is knowledgeable about how to conduct himself professionally. Any business savvy person would not do business with the other two individuals. Their character and attitude tells a lot about how they handle business.

## *"Many People Take Advice, But Only The Wise Will Profit From It"*

Have you ever received business advice at a seminar, boot camp, conference, or just out in a local public places where professionals congregate and network such as Panera Bread or Starbucks? Did you take the advice given to you and run with it? In other words, did you make a profit off of it? There's actually an art to taking advice, the advice you soak in could be the very next thing you use to start growing your business. Find opportunities to soak in value from others, think about how you're going to serve people with it as well as how you can capitalize on it.

Never waste talent because it will stay with you if you use it properly and it will line up with your purpose. Skills, talent, and purpose are three different things. Let's take a look at what these three things are: Skills are learned from doing something consistently, everyone you associate with has some type of skill. It can be writing, speaking, dribbling a ball, or even being a sales person. Many people have various skills and are known for doing all of them very well. However, everyone who has a skill may not want to use that skill to make a living because it does not align with their purpose.

I'm sure you're asking, "How do I identify my talents?" and "How do I find my purpose?" Well, what are you good at; would you do for free every day, all day for the rest of your life? Will it help others, and can you capitalize on it? If you can figure that out, it's your passion and your purpose. For example, a person who has a talent for speaking, would do free speaking events, and have a vision of becoming a successful speaker, owning their own speaking business is passionate about speaking and should realize that it is their passion and their purpose.

How would you feel if you didn't share with the world the advice you took and experiences you learned from to make a profit? Taking advice and running with it takes the speaker from where he is now, to where he is destined to go – speaking at large conferences, events, and seminars around the globe. It's not about the profits, it's about how he is going to impact lives and give value to others who attend these events. If you're a new entrepreneur, it would serve you well to apply the information you just learned. Not new to the business world? Pass the information along to someone who is new and aspiring to shape their future.

Starting a business can be overwhelming, frustrating, and downright tiring. But it is worth it to see your vision appear right before your eyes. Never go at it alone, always consider logical business advice so that you may avoid mistakes others have made before you. And since I am certainly not the only business person with sound advice, I reached out to a few business associates in my network and asked for their advice for new entrepreneurs. These people include business experts, entrepreneurs, business owners, clients and great speakers - Below you will see their answers!

**Get to Know Your Partners**: Relationship building is the most important part of starting a business and sustaining it. Building great relationships help take your business to another level. Successful entrepreneurs understand that getting to know people are more important than just meeting people.

**Thanks to:** Juan Langford, (Professional Speaker, Business Coach)

**Become Unemployable:** If you start a process and it fails there is no plan B, there can be a plan B within plan A. Do whatever it takes to not work for someone else and build a business.

**Thanks to:** Gary Coxe, (Entrepreneur and Dynamic Speaker) www.GaryCoxe.com

**Do It Afraid:** Your dream, goal, and ambition of being an entrepreneur is going to be met head on with fear. Will it work? Will you make it? What will others think? My best advice is to do it afraid. Look fear in the eye and meet it head on. You won't have all the answers at first but you will learn. Zig Ziglar, said you don't have to be great to get started but you have to start to be great.

**Thanks to**: Tim Davis, (Business Coach and Speaker) www.TimDavisOnline.com

**You Are Your Message - Perfect It Daily:** When developing a business, especially as a speaker, you must work on leading yourself well before you can start and grow a business that involves leading others. Therefore, work on becoming the best you that you can be - an original - nothing less. Allow the way you live and conduct business to be the loudest message your audience will hear.

**Thanks to:** Lakeisha McKnight, (Award-Winning Entrepreneur and Speaker) www.lmcknight.com

**Know Your Target Market Inside and Out:** So many entrepreneurs do a great job of identifying their area of expertise by taking the time to gain industry knowledge in the beginning stages of their business. It is a big mistake to not know and understanding the true needs of your target market. You can have a great product, even offer a great service, but if your product or service does not meet the needs of your specific target market, then the likelihood of success is slim to none. Take the time to know who your target market is, where they are, what they need, and how you can meet that need. An entrepreneur's focus should always be to solve their customers' problems and/or meet their needs in a way their competitors cannot.

**Thanks to:** Yolanda Moore, (Two-time WNBA Champion, Author and Speaker) www.ymoore33.com


**The Power of Cash Flow:** For many of us who start a business, our goal is to accumulate and set aside as much money as possible. This is called managing cash flow, which is the most powerful financial concept in the world. *It is the amount of your cash flow, not your salary that will determine how successful you will be in life.* Cash flow is not simply your ability to make money, but also your ability to manage and multiply it. Again, the key is not how much you make, but how much of what you make is kept and not given to your creditors. At this point, you should be asking yourself, "What is cash flow and why is it so important?" Cash flow is simply your inflows (money from your business salary and assets) minus your outflows (debts, living expenses, and fun money). The difference in those two is what's called cash flow. *It's this number, and this number alone, that will determine the quality of your life.* Your decision to acquire assets is based on the cash flow you receive. Be mindful, you are not trying to purchase the most expensive asset or the property that is in the right neighborhood, but rather assets that produce cash flow. In life and in business, every single financial decision a person makes must be made in light of this question: *"HOW WILL THIS DECISION IMPACT MY CASH FLOW?"*

**Thanks To:** Vincent K. Harris, (Investor, Mentor, and Entrepreneur) www.VinceOnBusiness.com


**Be yourself when applying every piece of advice that's given to you so that you may become that consummate businessman or businesswoman you've always wanted to become. The future is yours!**

*Chapter 8*

# UNLOCK YOUR POTENTIAL

Progress equals promotion, and here we are with more steps to take to make sure you continue breaking the mold in life and business. So far, I hope I have inspired and pushed you to use everything you've been given for use in the entrepreneurial world. You can make a difference in this world with the decisions you make, the dedication you show, and the determination you have. Take this with you today as your move forward towards your destiny, *"Your dreams are seeds that live inside of you, just don't let them be buried with you."* This should change your thinking and inspire you to reach everything in life that you desire and work for.

Without a doubt, always be the person you want to MEET in life and in business. It's time to make a change and decide that you want to leave a Godly Legacy for years to come. Your achievement begins in your mind. The NBA was in someone's mind, Apple was in Steve Jobs mind, etc. You have to think outside the box forever, your quality of life will be more refreshing when you see the vision.

Even if it takes a while, it's better to reach your potential now before it becomes a much longer process later. Use your message to your advantage and for the advancement of others. How can a person change where they are going, before they change what they are looking at? It all comes with the way you view yourself. And that comes with your body language and the confidence you have.

You have to put into your mind that you're going to break the mold by doing things differently in a way that most people do not. Be diligent in your work and live by the attitude of "just do it," never give up on anything you believe in. I'm excited to know that you are willing to unlock every door in your life and utilize your potential. You need to succeed so that you will stand firm and grow your business, help someone in your family, and make a huge impact on the lives of many. You have a great mindset, just stay around other people who are dedicated to their future and who want to go really far in life.

Refer this book to the people you encounter every day, or give it to someone you know who needs to read it so they may be inspired to go after great things in life. I truly believe that it's not about creating more followers but about creating more leaders. It took me years to finally sit down and write this book, to tell the story of how I was a high school dropout and initially getting into college without a high-school diploma. What life taught me in general is that you have to lock in on your dreams. It does not matter what the naysayers think, say, or do, people will doubt your potential who only see you as the person you USED to be.

Don't let them slow down your progress, just keep pushing towards your ideal future and remember, *"Your future is created by what you do TODAY, not TOMORROW."* When you don't let the small things get to you, it simply means you're growing. Keep dreaming and moving forward, but move while you're dreaming so that you're able to unlock the potential that's on the inside of you. Surviving is not enough, you have to live your biggest dreams, make sure you don't waste talent, and BREAK THE MOLD.

## IMPLEMENTATIONS TO UNLOCKING YOUR POTENTIAL:

**Be Motivated:** You should be the first to rise each and every day, getting up before your family and friends. Without motivation you can't do it. Quiet the mind throughout your day, when you have a still mind you can do anything. Here are a few motivation tips:

- ✓ Say your daily affirmations before working on your plans
- ✓ Identify what it is you really want to accomplish, write them down on paper, and be as detailed as possible the steps you will take to finish every goal
- ✓ Write down who you want to help you achieve each goal and a deadline you expect to finish
- ✓ Seize your day and keep your mind focused

**Prioritize Time:** Putting your priorities in line is critical, you can't regain the time you've lost from being distracted.

- ✓ Whatever you feed the most grows the most, make sure you feed into your goals and dreams and watch how much they grow
- ✓ Act on your potential because I've learned that money loves speed from one of my best mentors
- ✓ Lay out your daily tasks by scheduling a certain time for each one

**Take Action:** Based off your list that you have prioritized, take action step-by-step so that you will start to see results from each action point.

**Unbelievable Focus:** Distraction and procrastination are two of the main reasons most people can't get anything done. Don't get me wrong, a long time ago I used to have trouble with focusing. But when I began to discipline myself, I started to see a lot of potential coming out of me. There are going to be distractions everywhere, (cell phones, cluttered environments, social media, TV, etc.) but to avoid lack of focus, you have to constantly tell yourself to stay on task.

**Personal Development:** In order to become the person you want to become, you have to change and work at being a better person. No one can change you, but YOU!!

**Self-Image/Posture:** How well you present and carry yourself tells a lot about you. Don't waste your potential by not having the correct posture. See yourself as a winner at all times. See yourself as already being successful and a finisher. For if you change the way you see yourself, you'll rise to a new level. You will never rise any higher than the image you have of yourself.

**Know Your Strengths and Weaknesses:** Some people do not know what their strengths and weaknesses are, you can find out by asking ten people who are close to you. However, I'm sure you have heard the saying, *"Be careful who you share your weaknesses with. Some people can't wait for the opportunity to use them against you."* You can't share all your weaknesses with certain people, some of them will try to use your weaknesses to stop you from growing. Be sure to work on them and have a different mindset towards your success.

## Chapter 9
# BREAKING THE CURSE

"You are the one that's going to have to break this curse," were the life-changing words little Christopher heard his aunt say to him – he didn't know what they meant at the time, but he did know it meant some kind of CHANGE.

One day he and his family were sitting on sofa in the living room, there were some familial issues being discussed and emotions were at their peak. There was a lot of confusion and Christopher could not understand just what was going on, but he wanted to know how he could help fix it. From that point on, he knew exactly what he had to do. Christopher needed to be the change his family needed. Have you ever heard of a self-fulfilling prophecy? Well, those words helped shape Christopher's future and the future of generations to come. He now understands that in order to break a cycle, you cannot accept the unfavorable as just a way of life. He also learned that complaining about and tolerating a situation can never change it. In essence, if you tolerate something you do not like, you are accepting it into your life. Tolerance vs. Acceptance, is there really a difference?

Until people realize there isn't any difference between the two and raise their standards, they will continue to wallow in mediocrity. Do you know someone who has always worked hard for their loved ones yet never really have enough to enjoy and do things in life? They pass this trait on to their offspring, and the trait is handed down onto the third and fourth generations. This is a generational curse; someone who recognizes the trend but doesn't do anything to stop it, doesn't desire change for future generations. Christopher was determined to break his generational curse.

The Bible mentions "generational curses" in several places. Namely, Exodus 20:5,34:7; Numbers 14:18; and Deuteronomy 5:9. God warns us that He is, "a jealous God, punishing the children for the sin of the fathers to the third and fourth generation of those who hate me." Do you think it sounds unfair for God to punish children for the sins of their fathers? Let's go back to the story of the little boy named Christopher. He was informed that he's going to have to be the one who breaks the curse

Most people aren't as fortunate to have that responsibility placed on them at such an early age. It gave Christopher enough time to self-fulfill that prophecy. Christopher seems to be the only one who has the spirit and ability to change his family's future. He's gifted and talented, and he doesn't want future generations to go through the same struggles of past generations whether it's personally, financially, or business related. He's determined to break the mold for generations to come, and has the desire to retire his parents when he makes it.

Throughout the years of seeing two sides of the world, the wealthy people and the poor ones, I decided that it is better to become wealthy so that you can lift others higher, and remove the bondage and baggage they carry in the lives. It should be in every man's heart to leave a Godly legacy for his children and their children. I encourage every young man and woman to leave this earth a better place for your family and for others. Wanting to break the mold is inspiration given by God and it starts in your mind. Where the mind goes, the body follows. Lead the path to where you want your body to go, and bring those with you who want to change their circumstances.

## Chapter 10

# WHY WASTE TALENT?

*"There is One Leadership Quality That Will Make or Break You, PURSUIT"*

## Challenge Your Intellect

I figured this concept out when I was drawing and painting at an early age. I started to feel like there was more potential inside of me and drawing and painting pictures didn't feed my passion. Being a creative person, I couldn't stay in a box, and live in a dimly lit world of boredom. As human beings, our minds need to be challenged, that's how they become sharper and more valuable to us. I simply wanted to challenge my intellect, so I left the class to fulfill my dreams.

## Keep Your Commitments

When finding something that captures your heart, something that aligns with your future, and gives you the urge to move on, be sure to stay committed to it. Passion is just like a relationship; if your man or woman doesn't show that they're committed, you will lose interest and begin searching for someone who will fulfill your desires. Likewise, stay committed to whatever you're passionate about so that you don't waste the talent that could change the world.

## Hold on to Responsibility

Trying to confine your talent is like putting locked bars on how far you can go. Remember, passion can take you places, therefore use them to the best of your ability. There were times when I took on huge projects and workloads because with my drive and ability, I knew that I could get the work done because I worked well under pressure. Has there ever been a time when you took on a responsibility then realized it was a last minute type of situation, but you had to get it done or else? We all have those moments at some point in our lives. But as long as you achieve favorable results, holding on to certain responsibilities is okay.

## Never Fail to Lead

While growing up in church and then becoming a young entrepreneur, I started to see a pattern. In business I learned that when you inspire people you inspire them for a *LIFETIME*. Songs in church, the environment, the congregation, the Pastor and saving souls are what grows the church and empowers people. That applies in business as well. When you lead a crowd they will tend to stay with you because they KNOW, LIKE and TRUST you. However, if you fail to lead correctly, your talent will find leadership in another place.

## Never Fail to Care

Emotions are what build people up or tear them down. . Throughout the course of life, many people fail to understand the difference between *"personal"* and *"business."* However, never fail to care for that individual because you can still be someone they respect and follow. Emotional levels differ, but if you plan to not care at all for people when doing business, they will eventually leave you. It doesn't matter what talents you have, gifts, money or freedom you can provide, because touching a heart first is always better than lending an insincere hand.

## Breakthrough to Your Passion

Some people have found their passion or something they love to do, but most people can't figure it out. There are successful people all around the world who have stayed locked inside their rooms with the door shut, and everything else didn't matter because they eliminated all distractions. When people can't seem to find something they are really passionate about, it makes me wonder if they ever had a mentor, or even been around driven people who will point out what they are talented at, can use to help others, and profit from it. You have to get to a certain point in your life where you realize you want to become better each day and become the greatest at what you do.

## Your Contributions

Having great mentors and soaking in their wisdom and advice, is critical to learning the ropes of business. One of my mentors explained to me the importance of staying under the radar. There are many people that would love to take all the credit, have all the fame, but that isn't what makes a great leader. A great leader gives his team all the credit for their hard work, loyalty, and diligence. Great businessmen are always under the radar doing business and still going after what they're passionate about. However they put together a team in place of qualified individuals who can get more of these things accomplished. It was once explained to me that the greatest man who walked this earth had a team of 12, so what makes us think we can do everything by ourselves?

When you don't recognize the contributions of others you're simply asking them to give you the credit and leave.

## That Inner Voice

Many entrepreneurs and business people have what it takes to win in this world by taking action on their thoughts, ideas, and insights. It's very few who really listen to that inner voice that gives them confirmation that it's time to make it happen. If you don't listen to that voice, I promise you someone else will.

## Discover Your Purpose

Have you discovered your purpose and what you're really supposed to do in life? Do you have a clear understanding of your calling? Many people go through life without finding their true purpose. You'll find what's right for you when doors begin to open or slam shut. Either way, when defining your purpose, you have to figure out who you ARE by what you are NOT.

*Chapter 11*

# MENTAL SUCCESS STRATEGIES

You may have heard the saying "you can lead a person to the well, but you can't make them drink," that's a true statement. I have heard many people say they have big dreams, but their actions show me otherwise. Reflect on the following mental strategies, take ownership of your success so far, and really start applying the knowledge you learn to your future actions.

**William E. Lee Jr.'s Mental Success Strategies:**

**Find Your Niche:**

Once you find what is best for you, it's always good to stay in your own lane and let your team of people use what works best with their gifts and talents. As entrepreneurs, never become a jack-of-all-trades but a master of none.

**Make Good Decisions:**

Surround yourself with people who are successful and already making good decisions. Understand that, *"You are equivalent of the 5 people you hang around the most."* People who are good resources for you will push you to the next level, and people who are liabilities will push you back to a previous level. Always make good decisions and have invaluable mentors in your circle.

**Be Legitimate:**

Always make sure you have your business set up properly so that nothing shows up and surprises you down the road. It's good to have a legal team and a team of consultants so that you're not trying to make decisions on your own. If you have a team of people who are specialized in their field and can give you the blueprint, you make an educated decision from there.

**Strive to Learn Everything There is to Know:**

I've heard this saying plenty of times, *"if you are the smartest person in the room, you are in the wrong room."* Now don't get me wrong, you may know a few things but you will never know everything there is to know. But it doesn't hurt to strive to know. As one of my mentors taught me, *"we have two ears and one mouth"* which makes it great to keep your ears open and lips closed. Learn everything you can, knowledge is great and it will promote you.

**Shorten your time from the TV:**

I'm sure you've heard this often but, *"there's a time and place for everything."* You can take that to the bank, because it is valuable information. Always shorten your time from watching television because it can become a distraction for most people. On a regular basis, I make sure that I don't have the TV on while I work, and if I do, I have the volume muted so that I won't be distracted.

**Become a Positive Thinker:** Avoid people who think negatively and surround yourself with people who lift you up with words. Instead of saying you can't do something, it's too much, or I don't have what I need. Find a way to think positively and say, "I have what it takes", I will find a solution to my problem", "I can do this."

## Chapter 12

# DAILY AFFIRMATIONS

Everything we think, hear, and say is an affirmation. Either you're speaking positive things into your life or negative things that will keep you stuck in a rut.

**What do you want in life or business?**

Take about 20 minutes of your time to look at your life and consider the things you currently believe. If you feel you are missing pieces of your life and/or business, write that belief down and speak into existence what it is you are missing. Doing this will create a positive belief to help your mind reprogram itself to create and accept abundance.

For example: Susan wants to change her mindset and start a business, although she isn't surrounded by positive people who support her vision, and who inspire her to go after her dreams. Susan believes it is time for a change and is ready to take massive action. To get started, she can listen to motivational audio daily and create a list of positive affirmations. A few affirmations she could use are listed below:

**Susan's Powerful Affirmations for Life & Business**

- ✓ Today, I have started my journey in creating my own business and taking massive action

- ✓ Every day I am changing my circle of friends, replacing them with people who see my potential and enlarging my territory
- ✓ I make sure I give the best by providing good value, service, and making sure every client is satisfied with my service
- ✓ I am persistent in my business decisions
- ✓ I am successful and lend help to those in need
- ✓ My business produces massive profits more and more each day
- ✓ I allow surplus in my steps
- ✓ I am focused throughout my day

Susan can create this simple list of affirmations for herself and repeat them aloud every single day without missing a beat.

## Powerful Change

Now you will start to experience a change in your thinking and a change your steps. Things will come easier to you because you're speaking positive things in the universe that gravitates to your commands. But you still must take action, I'm sure this is something you will not have a problem doing. All these changes are important in your life as they assure that you don't waste the talent that can take you to the next level in life.

I learned these things from one of my mentors, and now I say my positive affirmations at least three times a day:

- ✓ Every morning after I shower
- ✓ Before I start working
- ✓ At the end of the day or late at night

Remember, this is your moment, the peak of your season. Make a difference and prove it can be done by your decisions, dedication and determination. Improve your life, help others avoid mistakes, be different, and someone will want to sow seeds of growth into your life. Someone helped me, now I want to help you. Why Waste Talent?

Take care, Break the Mold
William

# ABOUT THE AUTHOR

William Lee is the founder of Lee Graphix PR and Design Group and a multitude of other businesses and nonprofits. He is a motivational speaker, graphic designer, entrepreneur, and most importantly, a Christian businessman who has a desire to inspire young adults across the globe.

In 2011, William was nominated, along with six additional great men, for the Just For H.I.M. Affair, and was blessed to be the recipient of the "Hardest Working Man in North Carolina" award. Understanding the hard work his fellow nominees put in and how they equally qualified to receive such an award, he was truly humbled and grateful for the recognition. William has since then dedicated his life to helping other aspiring entrepreneurs discover their passion and execute business ideas. He wrote, *"Breaking the Mold"* to teach young adults how to find their niche, become more influential, and use their number one passion to create a solid business model.

An influential entrepreneur himself, William delivers straight talk, inspiration, a story many can relate to, and motivation for all. He has been featured on the front cover of Genesis Magazine, which circulates in fourteen countries and an exclusive article in Greensboro LIVE. He has also worked with and helped many entrepreneurs and businesses, which include the following:

- ✓ **Larramie "Doc" Shaw** - Tyler Perry's House of Payne, Actor on Disney XD
- ✓ **Yolanda Moore** - Two-Time WNBA Champion
- ✓ **Vincent K. Harris** – Bestselling Author, Entrepreneur, Businessman, Speaker
- ✓ **Cee Cee Michaela** - The TV Show "Girlfriends" and the movie "Hair Show"
- ✓ **LaKeisha McKnight** - Entrepreneur, Author, Motivational Speaker
- ✓ **Odell A. Bizzell II** - Speaker, Author, Entrepreneur
- ✓ **Nola Catering** – Head Chef, Irvin J. Williams
- ✓ **Monique Pro Makeup** – Celebrity Makeup Artist
- ✓ **Shavon Reed-Agard** – Certified Life Coach, Speaker & Communication Consultant
- ✓ **Myles Munroe International** –International Outreach Ministries powered by Dr. Myles Munroe *and many more!!*

You can visit us online at www.LeeGraphixPR.com

William, a young businessman, has been called with a purpose to help others avoid mistakes and live a life of value. He was the first in his family to attend college, and has mentored and counseled youth in the community. William's mission is to leave a Godly Legacy for future generations.

Inspiring and motivating young adults play a major part in his life because of the road he previously traveled. His message resonates with others because he understands, it does not matter what you did in your past; anyone can make a significant change. William believes, *"Your future is created by what you do TODAY, not TOMORROW!"*

William is available for: Conferences, Career Day, High School Pep Rallies, One-on-One Mentoring, Church Events and much more!! Email: booking@williamleeonline.com

Please submit all business inquiries: william@williamleeonline.com

## *The Future is YOURS!!*
## www.WilliamLeeOnline.com